THE OUTSIDERS

by
S. E. Hinton

Teacher Guide

Written by
Linda Herman

Note

The 2008 Speak paperback edition of the novel, © 1967 by S. E. Hinton and renewed 1995, was used to prepare this guide. Page references may differ in other editions. Novel ISBN: 978-0-14-038572-4

Please note: This novel deals with sensitive, mature issues. Please assess the appropriateness of this novel for the age level and maturity of your students prior to reading and discussing it with them.

ISBN 978-1-56137-362-8

To order, contact your local school supply store, or—

Novel Units, Inc.
P.O. Box 97
Bulverde, TX 78163-0097

Web site: novelunits.com

Table of Contents

Skills and Strategies

Comprehension
Creative thinking, identifying attributes, inferences, problem solving, predictions, supporting judgments

Critical Thinking
Analysis, brainstorming, cause/effect, compare/contrast, evaluation, research

Literary Elements
Character analysis, conflict, story mapping, theme, author's purpose, figurative language, point of view

Writing
Creative writing, dialogue, essay, personal narrative, poetry, report, diary entry, newspaper editorial, menu, biography

Vocabulary
Definitions, word maps, slang, compound words, target words

Listening/Speaking
Discussion, dramatization, oral presentation, debate, interview

Across the Curriculum
Social Studies—stereotypes, gang culture, history, rodeo, juvenile justice system, runaways, bullying; Health—psychology, family relationships, daydreaming, self-worth; Math—budgeting; Art—illustration, design, poster, model; Literature—Robert Frost; Music—time line, soundtrack; Film—*Gone with the Wind, The Outsiders*, James Dean

Genre: young-adult fiction

Setting: 1960s; the Southwest, presumably Tulsa, Oklahoma (the author's hometown)

Point of View: first person

Themes: isolation, identity, friendship, survival, self-esteem, society and class, relationships, violence, death, loyalty, honor, appearances, bullying, making choices, coming of age

Conflict: person vs. self, person vs. person, person vs. society

Style: narrative

Tone: candid, conversational, thought-provoking

Date of First Publication: 1967

Summary

Ponyboy Curtis feels like an outsider, both at home—where he can never seem to please his strict older brother—and with his friends the greasers, a gang of long-haired teens from the poor East Side. Though loyal to his gang, Ponyboy would rather watch sunsets and study than rumble with the Socs, the wealthy teens from the West Side. He does not understand why the Socs, who have everything, enjoy beating up greasers. Then he meets Cherry, a Soc girl, and learns that Socs have problems, too. Cherry's boyfriend and his friends attack Ponyboy and Johnny, the gang's most vulnerable member. Johnny kills Cherry's boyfriend in self-defense. With the help of Dally, the greasers' toughest member, Ponyboy and Johnny hide out in an abandoned church. The church later catches on fire, trapping schoolchildren inside. Ponyboy and Johnny rush into the burning building and rescue the children, but Johnny is fatally wounded. When Johnny dies, a distraught Dally pulls an unloaded gun on police and is shot and killed. Unable to accept his friends' deaths, Ponyboy's life falls apart. Then, Ponyboy finds a letter Johnny wrote stating that saving the children was worth sacrificing his life. Johnny also encourages Ponyboy to value the good things in life, to become the person he wants to be, and to convince the hardened Dally to do the same. It is too late for Dally, but Ponyboy believes he might be able to help numerous underprivileged boys living on the wrong sides of other cities—society's outsiders. Ponyboy decides to write his story from the greasers' perspective for his upcoming English assignment, and so he begins writing *The Outsiders*.

About the Author

Susan Eloise Hinton was born in Tulsa, Oklahoma. At the age of ten, inspired by her love of reading, she began writing stories about cowboys and horses. She wrote *The Outsiders* while attending Will Rogers High School in Tulsa. Her publisher, concerned that male critics and readers would not accept a gang story written by a female, suggested publishing under the name S. E. Hinton. In 1970, Hinton received a B.S. in Education from the University of Tulsa. She followed *The Outsiders* with four young-adult novels—*That Was Then, This Is Now* (1971), *Rumble Fish* (1975), *Tex* (1979), and *Taming The Star Runner* (1988)—all of which share the same setting and themes and were named Best Books for Young Adults by the American Library Association. All but *Taming The Star Runner* were made into films with Hinton consulting and occasionally playing cameo roles. She co-wrote the screenplay for *Rumble Fish* with Francis Ford Coppola. Hinton also wrote two children's books, *Big David, Little David* (1995) and *The Puppy*

Sister (1995), before turning to adult books with *Hawkes Harbor* (2004) and a collection of stories titled *Some of Tim's Stories* (2007). In 1988, Hinton was honored as the first recipient of the annual Margaret A. Edwards Award, which recognizes authors for a "significant and lasting contribution to young adult literature" that helps adolescents become aware of themselves and their roles in life. Hinton's novels, especially the classic *The Outsiders*, made her a pioneer in realistic young-adult fiction and earned her the title "The Voice of the Youth."

Background Information

S. E. Hinton wrote *The Outsiders* because of the social situation in her high school. She felt that realistic young-adult fiction did not exist at the time, only what she calls "Mary-Jane Goes to The Prom" novels. A classmate's real-life experience inspired *The Outsiders'* opening scene. Though not a Soc or a greaser, Hinton was a tomboy who identified with the greasers in her neighborhood and chose to tell the story from their viewpoint. She admits her "alter ego is clearly a 15-year-old boy."

The Outsiders has sold over 14 million copies and is required reading in many schools. Hinton credits the novel's popularity to the fact that everyone knows the feeling of being an outsider. She also believes the Oklahoma setting is "closer to the universal experience than it would be if I wrote it from L.A. or New York. It's an everyman story." The novel, however, is often banned or challenged for being inappropriate for teens because of its depiction of gang violence and glamorization of smoking, drinking, and swearing.

As Ponyboy points out in the novel, his gang is a group of friends, not a gang like the organized ones that Dally associated with in New York. Greasers still exist today; however, their heyday was in the 1950s and 1960s, when they were famous for greased-back hairstyles, leather jackets, hot rod cars, and rockabilly music. The greaser culture gained popularity through films such as *The Wild One* (1953), *Rebel Without a Cause* (1955), *American Graffiti* (1973), and *Grease* (1978) and became a symbol of rebellious youth.

Characters

Ponyboy (Pony) Michael Curtis: greaser; 14-year-old boy with light-brown hair and greenish-gray eyes; enjoys reading and watching sunsets; tough and loyal but questions violence; eventually realizes that he does not have to remain an outsider

Sodapop (Soda) Patrick Curtis: greaser; Ponyboy's 16-year-old brother; handsome with long, straight, dark-gold hair; outgoing and lively; high-school dropout who is happy working at a gas station; mediates between Ponyboy and Darry

Darrel (Darry) Shaynne Curtis, Jr.: greaser; Ponyboy's 20-year-old brother; tall and muscular with dark-brown hair; tough, athletic, and smart; would be a Soc if not for the responsibility of supporting his brothers after their parents' deaths

Johnny Cade: greaser; small, sensitive 16-year-old from an abusive home; Ponyboy's closest friend; "the gang's pet" (p. 12); dies from injuries sustained while saving children from a fire

Dallas (Dally) Winston: greaser; blond-haired, blue-eyed 17-year-old; angry and hateful; toughest and most dangerous member of Ponyboy's gang; associated with organized gangs in New York and has been in and out of jail since he was ten years old; loves, protects, and dies for Johnny

Steve Randle: greaser; Soda's 17-year-old best friend; tall and lean; works with Soda at the gas station; specializes in repairing (and stealing) cars

Keith (Two-Bit) Mathews: greaser; tall, stocky 18-year-old; jokester; alcoholic; known for shoplifting and his black-handled switchblade

Tim Shepard: greaser; lean and intense; leader of an organized gang

Sherri (Cherry) Valance: Soc; attractive redhead; Bob's girlfriend; connects with Ponyboy; helps the greasers

Marcia: Soc; Cherry's friend; Randy's girlfriend

Robert (Bob) Sheldon: Soc; spoiled; drives a blue Mustang; wears rings; mean when drunk; Johnny kills him in self-defense.

Randy Adderson: Soc; Bob's best friend; confides in Ponyboy; chooses to stop fighting

Paul Holden: Soc; Darry's former friend and football teammate

Buck Merril: Dally's rodeo partner; tall, lanky cowboy; gambler and bootlegger

Jerry Wood: teacher in charge of the children caught in the church fire; grateful to Ponyboy and Johnny for their help

Mr. Syme: Ponyboy's English teacher; cares about his students realizing their full potential; gives the assignment for which Ponyboy writes *The Outsiders*

Initiating Activities

Use one or more of the following to introduce the novel.

1. Social Studies: As a class, brainstorm stereotypical terms associated with school groups, such as thug, preppy, jock, geek, bookworm, Goth, skater, etc. Have students discuss how stereotypes can influence and affect people.

2. Social Studies: Ask students to determine the definition of a "gang." As a class, make a list of reasons why a teenager might join a gang.

3. Creative Writing/Social Studies: Discuss with students the meaning of the term "non-traditional family." Have students write a brief essay in which they discuss their opinions on the following topics: What characteristics describe a good parent or guardian? Can an older sibling be a good guardian? Can a group of friends take the place of a family?

4. History: Tell students that *The Outsiders* takes place during the 1960s. Students should research major news stories from the era (e.g., JFK and RFK assassinations, Civil Rights Movement, Cuban Missile Crisis, Vietnam War, Space Race, Beatlemania) and present their findings.

5. Predictions: Have students complete the I Predict… activity on page 27 of this guide. Give students the following thematic clues, and ask them to make additional predictions on a separate sheet of paper: appearances, friendship, loyalty, honor, bullying, violence, and self-esteem.

Vocabulary Activities

1. Visual Vocabulary: Divide the class into two teams. Have students from each team take turns illustrating assigned vocabulary words. Set a time limit, and have the chosen student's team guess the word. After the time limit, the other team has a chance to guess if the first team failed. Each team earns one point for a correct guess.

2. Word Map: Have students complete a Word Map (see page 28 of this guide) for ten vocabulary words from the lists in this guide.

3. Compound Word Match: Display the following words in two columns on a white board: Column #1—lone, foot, bill, head, cheer, out, hitch, sand; Column #2—quarters, fold, some, leader, paper, hiked, ball, casts. Have students combine the words to form compound words from the novel. Challenge students to list additional compound words as they read. (Answers: cheerleader, football, sandpaper, headquarters, hitchhiked, billfold, lonesome, outcasts)

4. Target Word Story: Instruct students to write an original short story using the following vocabulary words from the lists in this guide: unfathomable, hoodlum, sophisticated, premonition, eluded, exploits, conformity, idolized.

5. Slang Words: List the following words from *The Outsiders* on the board: lift, hood, fuzz, trap, dig, rumble. Instruct students to write two sentences for each word—one that shows the slang meaning and one that shows the formal meaning of the word.

Chapters 1–2

Ponyboy Curtis leaves the local movie theater and is jumped by a rival gang, the West-side rich kids known as the Socs. Ponyboy's gang, called "greasers" like all of the low-income kids living on the East Side, arrives in time to save Ponyboy from a severe beating. Johnny Cade, Steve Randle, Two-Bit Mathews, and Dally Winston chase away the Socs while Ponyboy's older brothers, Darry and Soda, look after him. The next night at the drive-in movies, Johnny uncharacteristically stops Dally from harassing Cherry and Marcia, two Soc girls. Cherry, a cheerleader, tells Ponyboy that not all Socs are bad and that Socs have problems, too.

Vocabulary
asset
reckless
sympathetic
irresistibly
unfathomable
rivalry
suspicious
savvy
sarcasm
hoodlum
incredulous
nonchalantly
bickering
feud
stricken
vaguely
rebellious

Discussion Questions

1. Why does Ponyboy feel like an outsider? Why do you think he walks home alone when he knows it is unsafe? *(Ponyboy is different than his brothers and the other members of the gang. He enjoys being alone, watching movies, and reading books. Ponyboy also feels isolated from society because greasers are considered low-class hoods. Answers will vary. Ponyboy enjoys walking and admits he does not always use his best judgment. He may also be acting rebellious.)*

2. Compare and contrast the Socs and greasers. Which group seems more dangerous? *(Socs—the West-side rich kids—jump greasers, wreck houses, and throw "beer blasts" for fun. Greasers—the East-side low-income kids—steal, rob gas stations, and are occasionally involved in scuffles. The Socs can be considered a public disgrace but still be favored by society; the greasers are considered criminals. Answers will vary. Some students may feel the two groups are equally dangerous. Others may feel the greasers are hoodlums, or true criminals. Still others may note that the Socs attack a less fortunate, outside group, while the greasers fight only among themselves. Discussion could also include the greasers' fair fight policy versus the Socs' use of weapons and habit of ganging up on a weaker person.)*

3. What does Darry mean when he asks Ponyboy, "You must think at school, with all those good grades you bring home…but do you ever use your head for common sense" (p. 13)? Do you think it is more important to have a good education or common sense? Explain your opinion. *(Ponyboy demonstrates his intelligence at school but not on the streets. He knows walking alone is not smart yet does so anyway and ends up in trouble. Answers will vary.)*

4. Describe Ponyboy's relationships with his brothers. Why does he feel closer to Soda than to Darry? *(Ponyboy loves Soda more than anyone because Soda makes him laugh, tries to understand him, and defends him. Soda is closer in age to Ponyboy and is the happy-go-lucky type whom everyone likes. Ponyboy is in awe of Darry, yet he also fears him. Darry has a serious personality. He is weighed down with the responsibility of supporting the family and serves as a father to Ponyboy. Ponyboy thinks Darry is overprotective and feels like he can never please him.)*

5. What is the difference between a greaser and a hood? Why is Dally more like a hood? *(Greasers form gangs of friends who protect each other. Hoods form organized gangs that are involved in criminal activities. Dally spent three years with the hoods of New York and has a criminal record. He hates the world and uses violence to vent his anger. Dally goes out of his way to defy authority.)*

6. What is Johnny's position in the gang? What does the gang mean to him? Why? *(Johnny is "the gang's pet, everyone's kid brother" [p. 12]. Protecting Johnny gives the gang a sense of purpose. The gang substitutes for Johnny's family, providing the only love and affection he receives. At home, Johnny's father beats him and both parents ignore him.)*

7. Ponyboy relates to Pip in *Great Expectations*, yet he says greasers "deserve a lot of [their] trouble" (p. 16). Explain what Ponyboy means. Do you think Ponyboy and the gang should attempt to fit into society or be themselves? *(Answers will vary. Like the character in the novel, Ponyboy does not like being looked down upon. He wants to fit in with his classmates in the "A classes." However, Ponyboy understands that the greasers' actions perpetuate their poor reputation.)*

8. Why do you think Ponyboy lies to himself? Is using an "unreliable narrator" an effective way to tell a story? *(Answers will vary. Ponyboy lies to avoid facing his true feelings, especially unpleasant feelings. Readers experience stories through narrators' perspectives; therefore, an unreliable narrator may seem ineffective. However, the author uses other characters to make readers aware of what Ponyboy misses or does not understand. For example, Soda's explanation about Darry's strictness makes readers aware that Ponyboy does not realize the truth about Darry's love. Unreliable narrators can add interesting twists to storytelling.)*

9. What can you infer about Dally from his harassment of Cherry and Marcia? Why do you think Johnny stops him, even though Johnny is usually unassertive? *(Answers will vary. Dally talks crudely to embarrass the girls and to show off. He disregards social propriety and derives pleasure from making the girls as uncomfortable as possible. He may also use what he considers tough behavior to hide his own feelings of inadequacy, setting up an excuse for the girls' rejection of him. Students should discuss whether Dally's interest in the Soc girls is simply because he enjoys bothering Socs whenever possible or because he likes one or both of them. Johnny probably stops Dally out of embarrassment and because he knows how it feels to be bullied.)*

10. Why does Ponyboy believe that "You take up for your buddies, no matter what they do" (p. 26)? Do you agree with him? Discuss any circumstances that might change your opinion. *(According to Ponyboy, gang members must stick together like brothers; otherwise, the gang will become a dangerous, distrustful pack like the Socs and New York street gangs. Answers will vary. Discussion should cover the pros and cons of being loyal and whether loyalty should be unconditional.)*

11. Why might Cherry admire Dally, and why doesn't she want anyone else to know this? *(Answers will vary. Cherry probably admires Dally because he says and does what he wants, even if it is frowned upon or illegal. As a Soc girl, Cherry is expected to behave properly and is unable to really be herself. Cherry senses a certain freedom in Dally, and she most likely wishes she could live that way. However, she can't let anyone know how she feels because it would compromise her reputation among the Socs and leave her vulnerable to the greasers.)*

12. How did the attack of four months ago affect Johnny? Why did Dally, who witnessed murders in New York, look sick when he saw Johnny after the attack? *(Johnny, who was already nervous due to conditions at home, became even jumpier after the attack. Though normally law-abiding, he began carrying a six-inch switchblade, ready to kill the next person who attacks him. Johnny wasn't affected by the physical pain of the attack as much as he was affected by the fear it instilled in him. Answers will vary. Dally cares about Johnny more than he did the New Yorkers. Dally's sick expression at Johnny's condition indicates how much Johnny means to him.)*

13. Why do you think Ponyboy tells Cherry about the Socs' attack on Johnny? What is significant about Cherry's reaction? *(Answers will vary. Ponyboy usually avoids thinking about the attack but unburdens himself to Cherry because she is not part of his gang. Cherry looks sick after Ponyboy describes the attack, which foreshadows that she knows who beat Johnny. It may also be an indication of her aversion to fighting, showing that she is someone Ponyboy can trust. However, she remains loyal to the Socs and does not reveal the attacker's identity. Instead, she tells Ponyboy that Socs have problems, too and that "things are rough all over" [p. 35].)*

14. **Prediction:** What are the possible consequences of Ponyboy and Cherry's relationship?

Supplementary Activities

1. Personal Narrative: At one time, Ponyboy thought he was the only person in the world who liked books and movies. Write about a time you've felt alone because of something you enjoy doing.

2. Comprehension: Ponyboy relates to Pip from *Great Expectations*. Choose a character from a novel that is most like you, and explain your choice in a brief essay.

3. Art/History: Design a photo essay or other artistic impression that illustrates the history of the rodeo. Explain the meaning behind your artwork and how it reflects the history and culture of the Southwest.

4. Critical Thinking: Ponyboy observes, "…we don't mind being called greaser by another greaser" (p. 28). Write an essay about why group members would call each other by a derogatory name. Explain whether you think this practice is beneficial or harmful and why groups might take offense to "outsiders" using the same derogatory names. Include possible effects on people outside the group.

Chapters 3–4

After the movie, Ponyboy and Cherry confide in each other. They determine that in some ways Socs and greasers are the same but have different values. Cherry's boyfriend Bob drives up with his friends in a blue Mustang. To avoid a fight, Cherry and Marcia leave with Bob and Randy. Ponyboy runs away when Darry slaps him for coming home late. At the park, Bob, Randy, and three other drunken Socs jump Ponyboy and Johnny. Ponyboy almost drowns, and Johnny kills Bob in self-defense. They run to Dally for help, and Dally gives them a gun and money and tells them to hide in an abandoned church in the country.

Discussion Questions

1. Analyze Cherry's statement that it is more than just money that separates greasers and Socs. What does Cherry mean when she says, "You greasers have a different set of values" (p. 38)? *(By acting sophisticated, Socs suppress their feelings to the point of becoming cold and unfeeling. Greasers, on the other hand, are emotional, sometimes too violently. Answers will vary. Both groups value their reputations. However, Socs focus on materialistic things to boost their status, while greasers make statements with their tough appearance and actions. Socs, caught up in the "rat race," lose sight of the important things in life and simply desire more. Life's hardships lead the greasers to value what is important in life: friendships, family, and loyalty to their gang.)*

Vocabulary
gallantly
sophisticated
aloofness
impersonally
elite
winced
cunning
resignedly
unceasingly
apprehensive
defiance
contemptuously
ruefully
bewildering
reformatory
premonition

2. What is Ponyboy telling Cherry when he says, "Just don't forget that some of us watch the sunset too" (p. 46)? *(Answers will vary. Though ashamed that Cherry will not acknowledge him at school, Ponyboy realizes they belong to different social classes and are expected not to associate. However, Ponyboy wants Cherry to understand that they do have some things in common and that not all greasers are violent and tough. He is reminding her of the connection they made and that, in some ways, all people are the same.)*

3. Why do you think Cherry believes that she could fall in love with Dally? *(Answers will vary. Cherry knows Dally behaves crudely and can be dangerously mean, yet she is oddly attracted to his "bad boy" nature. Cherry sees Dally's pride and respects his defiance and bravery. Dally is handsome and charming in his arrogance. Cherry may also be jealous of how "free" Dally is and wish to share that with him.)*

4. Review how each gang member deals with difficult circumstances and the social inequality with the Socs. Whose method do you think is best? Why don't any of these methods work for Ponyboy? *(Two-Bit accepts how things are without getting upset. Soda ignores the unfairness and loves life instead. Dally hardens himself until he no longer cares. Tim Shepard enjoys the excuse to fight with the Socs. Johnny wishes for a place with ordinary people who are not separated by class and do not fight each other. Ponyboy refuses to accept the unfairness, knowing that greasers should have the same rights as Socs. Answers will vary. Intelligence and education may have taught Ponyboy to think logically, to search for ways to correct injustice, and to strive for more in life.)*

5. Why does Johnny feel that the gang cannot replace a caring family? Why might he prefer being hit by his father to being ignored by both his parents? *(Answers will vary. Johnny craves his family's attention and considers negative attention better than none at all. Discussion should cover that while most teenagers prefer to spend time with friends, they still depend on parents for love and security.)*

6. Why do the Socs come after Ponyboy and Johnny? What does Ponyboy mean when he thinks, "[the Socs have] gone too far" (p. 56)? *(The Socs are retaliating because the greasers were talking to Cherry and Marcia at the movies. They probably feel insulted and embarrassed that the girls would rather talk to greasers than their own boyfriends. The Socs, especially Bob and Randy, are too angry or too drunk to stop at just beating up Johnny and Ponyboy. They are willing to drown Ponyboy.)*

7. Do you think Johnny meant to kill Bob? Did he have any other options? *(Answers will vary. Most students will believe Johnny killed Bob in self-defense and that, if he had not, he and Ponyboy would have died. Others may feel that because Johnny carries a switchblade, he was prepared to kill anyone who bothered him [especially since he had been severely beaten before].)*

8. Why do you think Johnny and Ponyboy go to Dally for help following Bob's death? *(Answers will vary. Johnny looks up to Dally, and Ponyboy is terrified to tell Darry what happened. The boys know that Dally will be willing and able to hide them. The boys believe that because of Dally's connections and his "criminal mind," he will know what to do. As Ponyboy remarks, he and Johnny believe "Dallas Winston could do anything" [p. 58].)*

9. Explain the irony of Johnny killing Bob. *(It is ironic that Johnny, the smallest, gentlest, shyest, and most law-abiding member of the gang, commits the most serious crime. The reader would expect Dally to be the gang member to kill a Soc.)*

10. Why doesn't Ponyboy like being in the country? What does he mean by, "There are things worse than being a greaser" (p. 65)? *(Eluding the police is much different than the idyllic country life Ponyboy had imagined. Contrary to his dreams, Ponyboy is away from his family and friends. He realizes that being a fugitive is worse than being a greaser.)*

11. **Prediction:** What does Ponyboy's "creepy feeling" in the church foretell?

Supplementary Activities

1. Comprehension/Writing/Art: Write a poem or create a collage depicting Cherry's questions to Ponyboy: "Did you ever hear of having more than you wanted? So that you couldn't want anything else and then started looking for something else to want" (p. 38)?

2. Art: Illustrate a sunset simultaneously viewed by two people with different perspectives.

3. Critical Thinking: Design a Web site to help teenagers who are thinking about running away from home. Include the causes and effects of running away as well as statistics on teen runaways.

4. Health: Ponyboy daydreams that his life would be better if he lived in the country. Research how daydreaming can affect a person's health. Then, lead a classroom discussion based on your findings.

5. Creative Writing: Choose one of the following, and write a dialogue between the characters: a) Darry and Soda discussing Ponyboy running away after Darry slaps him or b) Randy and the other three Socs discussing Bob's death.

Chapters 5–6

Ponyboy and Johnny reluctantly change their hair to disguise themselves. To pass the time, Ponyboy reads *Gone with the Wind* to Johnny, who compares the gallant Southern characters to Dally. Ponyboy also recites Robert Frost's poem, "Nothing Gold Can Stay." A week later, Dally takes them to a Dairy Queen, where Johnny announces his intention to turn himself in to the police. Returning to the church, they find the old building on fire with schoolchildren trapped inside. Ponyboy and Johnny rescue the children. However, a falling beam breaks Johnny's back and Dally is burned pulling Johnny from the church. At the hospital, the boys are hailed as heroes. Ponyboy reconciles with Darry, realizing Darry's strictness comes from love.

Discussion Questions

1. Compare and contrast Ponyboy's and Johnny's reactions to hiding in the old church. Why do you think Johnny takes the lead? *(Ponyboy falls asleep every chance he gets and, when he is awake, either pretends Bob's death did not occur or allows his overactive imagination to make the situation worse. Johnny plans and then takes action, making sure they reach the church and have supplies and the means to disguise themselves. Both boys begin crying, Ponyboy because he is frightened and Johnny over the enormity of taking a human life. After this emotional release, both boys accept the circumstances and are ready to face whatever happens next. Answers will vary. Johnny accepts sole responsibility for killing Bob and acknowledges he will be forever changed. He realizes that Ponyboy should be home with his family instead of hiding out with him.)*

Vocabulary
imploringly
sullenly
hue
subsides
eluded
fiend
indignant
gorged
doggedly
conviction
detached
keeled
inhalation
plasma
hysterics
racking

2. What is the significance of greasers' hair? Do you think appearance is important? Why or why not? (*Greasers cannot afford designer clothes to identify themselves; instead, they identify by their long, greased hair. Ponyboy, in particular, takes pride in his hair being similar to Soda's, since he idolizes his good-looking brother. Answers will vary.*)

3. How do Johnny and Ponyboy relate books to Dally? Explain how and why they view Dally differently. (*Johnny compares Dally to the gallant Southern gentlemen in* Gone with the Wind. *He considers Dally heroic—much like the Confederate soldiers facing death in the Civil War—for taking the blame for Two-Bit breaking school windows. Ponyboy associates heroes in novels with certain members of the gang but certainly not Dally. To Ponyboy, Dally is frighteningly real. Answers will vary. Johnny idolizes Dally, perhaps because Dally also survived a dysfunctional home. Johnny may wish that he was as tough and brave as Dally. Ponyboy only sees Dally as a criminal. Unlike the other gang members, Dally does not follow others. He charges ahead in life, unconcerned with the consequences.*)

4. Analyze and interpret Robert Frost's poem, "Nothing Gold Can Stay" (p. 77). How might the poem apply to *The Outsiders*? (*Answers will vary. The poem may simply be a description of nature's cycle, from budding leaves in springtime to their death in winter. The poem may also be providing a metaphor for the life cycle of humans—adults eventually lose their childhood innocence, essentially suffering a small "death." The poem implies that all golden, or good things such as youth, last only a short time. Circumstances such as poverty and violence force the novel's characters to become hardened, sometimes turning sensitive youths into criminals. The poem may express the greasers' feeling of hopelessness, or it may offer a message that all humans need to strive to live "golden," or meaningful, lives. The poem also seems to express the sentiment to appreciate things while one has them [i.e., while times are "golden"].*)

5. What effect does Bob's death have on the greasers and Socs' relationship? Evaluate Dally's decision to carry an unloaded gun. (*Throughout the city, greasers and Socs are at war. A war council has been held and a rumble scheduled to determine whether the Socs will continue to invade the greasers' territory. Answers will vary. Discussion could cover whether students believe Dally has a right to defend himself and his friends [if only by scare tactics] and if their opinions would change if Dally's gun were loaded.*)

6. What does Ponyboy mean when he thinks, "No, it wasn't Cherry the Soc who was helping us, it was Cherry the dreamer who watched sunsets and couldn't stand fights" (p. 86)? Do you agree with Cherry and Dally that Bob's death was Cherry's fault? (*Cherry views the increasing tension and violence from the perspective of an individual, not as a member of the Socs or even as Bob's girlfriend. She is responding to the situation based on her own decency and sense of what is right. Answers will vary. Some students may believe Cherry and Marcia should have known better than to associate with greasers, especially with their boyfriends' drinking issues. Others may feel that the girls have the right to talk to whomever they want and that Bob and the other Socs should have had the self-control not to react violently.*)

7. What does Dally talk about that surprises Ponyboy? Does Ponyboy's opinion of Dally change? *(Dally talks about how jail hardened him and how he does not want that to happen to Johnny. Ponyboy thought Dally did not care about anyone but himself. Hearing Dally express concern for Johnny allows Ponyboy to glimpse the person Dally might have been under different circumstances. Ponyboy imagines a ten-year-old Dally in jail and realizes Dally became a callous criminal to protect himself both physically and emotionally.)*

8. Why aren't Ponyboy and Johnny scared to run into the burning church? *(Answers will vary. Ponyboy and Johnny feel obligated to help the children because they assume their cigarettes started the fire. However, both boys seem unafraid because, for the first time since Bob's death, they have a purpose more important than their own safety. Students should note that determination and focus replace the usual "defeated, suspicious look" [p. 92] in Johnny's eyes.)*

9. How is Jerry Wood important to the story? *(Answers will vary. The teacher is the first person who is not a greaser to truly praise Ponyboy, Johnny, and Dally as heroes. Jerry does not care that the boys are greasers or that they are in trouble with the law. He reassures Ponyboy that the boys' heroic actions and self-defense explanation will sway the case in their favor. Telling Ponyboy that he is too young to smoke, something Ponyboy never considered, may help Ponyboy think about making choices in life rather than following what everyone else does.)*

10. What does Ponyboy mean by "I had taken the long way around, but I was finally home" (p. 99)? Have you ever misjudged a loved one's intentions? *(Answers will vary. Ponyboy admits he refused to see Darry's love, that he misread his brother's intentions and pushed him away. Darry, who did not cry at his parents' funeral, cries at the thought of losing his youngest brother. Ponyboy finally realizes that Darry loves him and is hard on him because he only wants what is best for him.)*

11. **Prediction:** How will the rest of the gang deal with news of Johnny's injuries?

Supplementary Activities

1. Math: Review the week's supplies Johnny purchases at the store. Research food prices at a grocery store, and then plan menus for one week of meals. Keep the cost as low as possible, and make sure your meals are nutritious and do not require refrigeration.

2. Creative Writing: Write a poem about hair representing social status. Your poem may be serious or humorous.

3. Film: View the movie *Gone with the Wind*. Identify which scenes you think best depict Southern charm and gallantry, and explain your choices.

4. Biography: Write a brief biographical sketch of Robert Frost. Include a paragraph about his poetry.

5. Comprehension: Rewrite the church fire scene from Johnny's point of view. Explain why Johnny looks as if "he was having the time of his life" (p. 92).

Chapters 7–8

Dally's burns are not serious; however, Johnny is in critical condition. Cherry and Randy publicly state that the Socs started the fight that resulted in Bob's death. Ponyboy discovers that he must attend a juvenile court hearing for running away and may be removed from his home. Randy confides to Ponyboy that he does not want to fight in the upcoming rumble. Two-Bit and Ponyboy visit Johnny and Dally in the hospital. Johnny asks for another copy of *Gone with the Wind* to replace the copy lost in the church fire, and Dally asks to borrow Two-Bit's black-handled switchblade. On the way home, Cherry informs Two-Bit that the Socs agree to fight without weapons, and then she talks to Ponyboy about Bob's positive qualities.

Vocabulary
mimicking
palomino
radiates
critical
bleak
mourning
delinquents
manslaughter
brawn
recurring
aghast
exploits
faltered
resemblance
divert

Discussion Questions

1. What does Darry mean when he tells the doctor that he, Soda, and Ponyboy are "about as much family as Dally and Johnny [have]" (p. 102)? *(Answers will vary, but students should note that Dally's and Johnny's parents do not care about their sons. The gang provides the security and love to Dally and Johnny that their parents do not.)*

2. Ponyboy panics at the thought of Johnny being crippled for life. Why does this cause Ponyboy to wish he is dreaming? How would being crippled be worse for Johnny than someone else? *(Ponyboy hopes he is dreaming because he cannot accept reality. He does not want to face the seriousness of Johnny's injuries. Johnny would not only have to deal with the trauma and difficulties of being crippled, but he would also be stuck at home where he is treated as if he is not wanted. He would be at his abusive parents' mercy, unable to defend himself or leave.)*

3. What does chocolate cake symbolize for Ponyboy, Soda, and Darry? *(Answers will vary. Chocolate cake seems to symbolize the bond between Ponyboy and his brothers. Despite their differences, Darry, Soda, and Ponyboy all love chocolate cake, which creates unity and provides comfort in their home. Chocolate cake may also remind them of better times with their parents. Darry may allow cake for breakfast to ease the pain of losing their parents or to bring about memories of their parents, since the boys' mother would never have allowed cake for breakfast.)*

4. Why is the door to Ponyboy's house always unlocked? Do you think this is wise? *(The Curtis house serves as a refuge for the gang and others like Tim Shepard when they have no place to go. Darry believes the risk of burglary is worth keeping the boys from staying out all night and causing trouble. Answers will vary.)*

5. The newspaper headline reads: "JUVENILE DELINQUENTS TURN HEROES" (p. 107). Why does Two-Bit think Ponyboy, Johnny, and Dally have always been heroes? *(Answers will vary. Two-Bit sees the good in others and knows his friends are decent people who have always had the capability to help others.)*

6. What is the significance of Ponyboy's nightmares? Why do they make Darry fearful? *(Answers will vary. The nightmares occur when Ponyboy is troubled, such as on the night of his parents' funeral. Darry worries that Ponyboy is stressed. He may also think the nightmares are a premonition that something bad is going to happen and may fear that the current nightmare foretells Ponyboy being sent to a boys' home.)*

7. Why do you think Sandy was sent to live with her grandmother? How does this affect Soda? *(Answers will vary. Students should infer that Sandy is pregnant and her parents will not allow her to get married at such a young age. Soda is miserable because he loves and misses Sandy.)*

8. What can you infer from Two-Bit's "outcast" joke? *(Answers will vary. Students should discuss whether Two-Bit really thinks that being a social outcast is helpful in life or if he's simply making jokes to mask his loneliness and discontentment.)*

9. Examine Randy's conversation with Ponyboy. What do the two boys teach each other? *(Ponyboy's hatred toward Socs diminishes after he understands what Cherry meant when she said Socs have problems, too. He realizes Randy is in pain and thinks fighting is futile, too. By telling Randy that running away won't help, Ponyboy acknowledges that inequality between social classes will always exist. Randy seems surprised and grateful for Ponyboy's different point of view. Randy thinks the world hates the wealthy but has to stop and think when Ponyboy says the wealthy hate the world. That Ponyboy would help a Soc and believes Randy is the type of person to risk his life to rescue children pleases Randy. Both boys learn that whether a Soc or a greaser, everyone is only human.)*

10. Analyze Randy's statement to Ponyboy: "[Bob] kept trying to make someone say 'No' and they never did…That was what he wanted. For somebody to…lay down the law, set the limits, give him something solid to stand on. That's what we all want, really" (p. 116). Do you agree with Randy's assertion? Why or why not? *(Answers will vary. Students should discuss the psychological benefits of parents setting boundaries and providing their children with structure and discipline, as well as how parents' actions and attitudes can affect a child's feelings of being safe and loved.)*

11. Discuss Johnny's mother's accusation that Ponyboy, Two-Bit, and the rest of the gang are to blame for Johnny's injuries. Do you think Johnny makes the right decision when he refuses to see his mother? *(Answers will vary. Discussion should compare the ways parents influence their children with the influence of friends. Some students may feel Johnny should have seen his mother in case she finally expressed love for him as he is dying. Most students will understand that Johnny realizes he will never receive his parents' love and he chooses not to face the heartbreak of another rejection.)*

12. Explain why Ponyboy believes Darry could easily be a Soc. Do you think Darry would rather be a Soc than a greaser? *(Answers will vary. Darry is smart and driven. He even has former friends among the Socs. If it weren't for custody of his brothers, he would probably continue his education and obtain a higher-paying job, perhaps even an athletic career. Darry would leave the East Side to make a better life for himself. Darry could have allowed Ponyboy and Soda to go to a boys' home when their parents died. Instead, he sacrificed his dreams to give Ponyboy the opportunity for a better life. Darry may not like being a greaser, but he loves his family.)*

13. **Prediction:** Why does Dally want Two-Bit's switchblade?

Supplementary Activities

1. Drama: Working in groups, reenact and record the scene in which Ponyboy and his brothers are in the hospital waiting room surrounded by TV reporters, police officers, and hospital staff.

2. Creative Writing: Soda reminds Ponyboy of a "long-legged palomino colt that has to get his nose into everything" (p. 101). Write a paragraph comparing your own personality to an animal.

3. Comprehension: Complete the Qualities of a Hero chart on page 29 of this guide for Ponyboy, Johnny, or Dally.

4. Critical Thinking: Make a list of the things you would like to do within the next five years. Then, create a written plan to accomplish your goals.

5. Comprehension: Write a diary entry from Cherry's point of view that describes her thoughts and feelings about Bob's death and its effect on the relationship between Socs and greasers.

Chapters 9–10

Ponyboy is ill but insists on participating in the upcoming rumble. Darry, representing the greasers, faces off against his one-time buddy, Paul, who represents the Socs. As the rumble begins, Dally arrives, having used Two-Bit's switchblade to threaten a nurse and escape from the hospital. When the Socs finally flee, Dally rushes Ponyboy to the hospital to see Johnny. Before he dies, Johnny says fighting is useless and tells Ponyboy to "stay gold." Dally breaks down and bolts from the hospital, leaving Ponyboy—who is dazed from a head injury he sustained in the rumble—to find his way home. The gang is devastated by the loss of Johnny but regroups when Dally calls for help after robbing a store. The gang arrives at the vacant lot in time to see Dally waving his unloaded gun at the police, who shoot and kill him. Ponyboy passes out and awakens several days later to find his exhausted brothers caring for him.

Vocabulary
wisecracks
mortal
grimacing
superiority
prime
menace
underprivileged
awed
conformity
leery
escort
raving
agony
stupor
impact
delirious

Discussion Questions

1. Analyze Ponyboy's parenthetical comments: "What kind of world is it where all I have to be proud of is a reputation for being a hood, and greasy hair? I don't want to be a hood, but even if I don't steal things and mug people...I'm marked lousy. Why should I be proud of it? Why should I even pretend to be proud of it?" (p. 132). *(Answers will vary. Ponyboy realizes that society often judges a person based on appearances rather than character or actions. Ponyboy is maturing and considering a more productive life. Note that it is not clear whether the text inserted in the parentheses represents Ponyboy's thoughts on the night of the rumble, or whether it is an aside to readers when he later writes* The Outsiders. *Ponyboy is either questioning his role as a greaser or commenting on how foolish he was that night.)*

2. Why do you think Ponyboy is determined to fight at the rumble when he believes self-defense is the only good reason to fight? *(Answers will vary. Ponyboy says, "Right then the most important thing in my life was helping us whip the Socs" [p. 134]. Loyalty to his gang overrides Ponyboy's personal feelings about fighting. Ponyboy understands that the gang members seek revenge against the Socs for causing events leading to Johnny's and Dally's injuries and that they want the Socs to stay out of their territory. Without Johnny, Dally, and Curly Shepard, the greasers are already at a disadvantage and therefore need Ponyboy to fight. Ponyboy sticks by his gang, despite his newfound respect for Cherry and Randy.)*

3. Ponyboy thinks: "Soda fought for fun, Steve for hatred, Darry for pride, and Two-Bit for conformity" (p. 137). Discuss each of Ponyboy's conclusions and whether each is justifiable as a reason for fighting. *(Answers will vary.)*

4. Why do Darry and Paul hate each other? *(Answers will vary. Suggestions: Paul feels contempt, pity, or hatred toward Darry, but his feelings are due to his being a Soc. For Darry, the hatred is personal. Darry may resent that his old buddy has the life he wanted for himself, or he may simply be angry that Paul no longer considers him a friend just because of their respective gang associations.)*

5. Do the greasers really win the rumble? *(Answers will vary. The Socs run away, acknowledging the greasers as victors. However, as Randy told Ponyboy earlier, nothing will change no matter who wins the rumble. The Socs will still be wealthy, and the greasers will still be disadvantaged. The hatred and diversity between the two groups will continue, as will challenges to future rumbles.)*

6. Examine Dally's speech to Ponyboy on the way to the hospital to visit Johnny (see page 147 of the novel). What might Dally be trying to tell Ponyboy? *(Answers will vary. Students should discuss whether Dally means what he says or if he is simply ranting out of grief for Johnny's condition and certain fate.)*

7. Analyze how the mood of the story changes throughout Chapter 9. *(At Ponyboy's house, the gang is excited, pumping themselves up for the rumble by performing acrobatics and chanting the slurs Socs use against them. Tension rises as the greasers wait for the Socs, and then fast-paced action occurs during the rumble. The drive to the hospital is portrayed hazily through Ponyboy's confusion. At the hospital, the mood is poignant. Dally shows tenderness to Johnny before his agony overtakes him and he bolts from the room.)*

8. What does Ponyboy mean when he says, "And this time my dreaming worked" (p. 150)? Why is his dreaming successful this time? *(Answers will vary. Stress compounded by injuries and illness overwhelm Ponyboy. Unable to accept the reality of Johnny dying, Ponyboy actually convinces himself that Johnny is not dead.)*

9. How would you describe Dally and Johnny's relationship? Why would Dally choose to die rather than live without Johnny? *(Answers will vary. Their relationship was codependent—Dally was someone Johnny could admire, and Johnny was someone Dally could protect. Johnny idolized Dally, wishing he were as brave as Dally. Johnny was the only thing in the world that Dally loved. Johnny's sensitive nature and vulnerability probably reminded Dally of himself before he was hardened by life on the streets. Dally and Johnny each possess characteristics the other lacks; however, they complement each other. Both boys come from homes where they are not wanted, so they turn to each other. Ironically, meek Johnny becomes stronger during the story while tough Dally falls apart. Dally considers himself Johnny's protector, yet he cannot protect Johnny from death. Johnny's death breaks through Dally's wall of self-preservation, and Dally is consumed by unbearable grief. He can no longer hide his emotions behind a tough attitude. Dally believes the only good thing in his life is gone and chooses to die rather than deal with his sadness and loss.)*

10. Explain Ponyboy's statement: "Dally didn't die a hero. He died violent and young and desperate…But Johnny was right. He died gallant" (p. 154). Do you agree with Ponyboy? Why or why not? *(Answers will vary. Dally chose to die the way he lived, harshly and violently. His loyalty extends only to the gang. In particular, he would do anything to protect Johnny. He willingly risks his life to help Johnny and Ponyboy after Bob's death and at the church fire. Unfortunately, Dally isn't strong enough to cope with losing Johnny. Some students may agree that Dally is gallant because he lived life fearlessly and upheld his principles. Others may feel that he acted cowardly when he raised a weapon at the police, knowing they would shoot him. Some students may even think that Dally acted selfishly, causing more pain to a group of friends who had already just suffered a great loss.)*

11. **Prediction:** What will happen to Ponyboy and Soda after the custody hearing?

Supplementary Activities

1. Art/Critical Thinking: Create a picture of Ponyboy's gang leaving the house on their way to the rumble. Compare and contrast your picture with those of classmates. Discuss whether similarities and differences come from details provided by the novel or from details filled in by readers' imaginations.

2. Biography/Art: Research James Dean. Write a brief biography of the actor, and (based on your research of Dean's life) create a poster advertising his movie, *Rebel Without a Cause*. How does this movie compare to *The Outsiders* (the novel)?

3. Literary Analysis: In slideshow format, create an illustrated character profile for Johnny or Dally. Your presentation should honor the character's brief life.

Chapters 11–12

Randy talks to Ponyboy about the events surrounding Bob's death. Ponyboy is acquitted at the court hearing but, unable to accept Johnny's and Dally's deaths, has difficulty returning to his normal life. When Ponyboy threatens three Socs with a broken bottle, Two-Bit tells him not to be tough, that he is different from the rest of the gang. Darry and Ponyboy argue, causing Soda to break down and reveal his true feelings about always being the middleman in their arguments. While searching for a theme for his English paper, Ponyboy discovers a letter from Johnny tucked inside *Gone with the Wind*. Johnny tells him to keep looking at the good in the world, to become who he wants to be, and to tell Dally to do the same. Ponyboy knows it's too late for Dally but thinks he can reach hundreds of other boys living on the wrong sides of their towns. Ponyboy begins writing *The Outsiders*.

Vocabulary
idolized
liable
guardian
flinching
acquitted
circumstances
reference
welled
vast

Discussion Questions

1. Why would Ponyboy rather have Bob's parents' hate than their pity? *(Answers will vary. Pity implies that Bob's parents consider themselves better than Ponyboy and the greasers. Ponyboy wants to be accepted for who he is, not considered a victim of his environment. Discussion could cover a detailed explanation of the meaning of "pity-the-victims-of-environment" [p. 162].)*

2. Ponyboy describes Bob as a "reckless, hot-tempered boy, cocky and scared stiff at the same time" (p. 162). Why does Ponyboy think Bob was scared? How does he now view Bob? *(Answers will vary. According to Randy, Bob only wanted discipline from his parents. Bob, perhaps as a cry for help, took drinking and fighting too far, which probably frightened him. Bob's egotism was most likely a front for his fear and uncertainty. Ponyboy now thinks of Bob as an individual and is able to imagine his thoughts. Discussion could cover whether Bob's parents let him run wild because they loved him too much or too little.)*

3. Explain the significance of Randy's concern upon learning that Ponyboy's parents are dead and that Ponyboy might be sent to a foster home. *(Answers will vary. Randy assumes that, like him, Ponyboy has parents who are disappointed in his behavior and that Ponyboy is ashamed for letting them down. Discovering Ponyboy does not have parents and may be taken from his brothers forces Randy to consider the hardships in others' lives. He realizes the far-reaching consequences of the Socs jumping Ponyboy and Johnny [e.g., Bob's death, Johnny's death, Dally's death, Ponyboy's legal troubles].)*

4. How does the doctor's conversation with the judge before the court hearing affect the proceedings? What do you think the doctor tells the judge? *(The judge does not ask Ponyboy any questions about Bob's death. He also does not mention Johnny or Dally while questioning Ponyboy. Answers will vary but should include that the doctor talked about Ponyboy's health. The doctor would explain that Ponyboy is not acting normal after suffering a head injury and is claiming to have killed Bob himself. He also may have advised the judge to refrain from mentioning Johnny or Dally.)*

5. Ponyboy is proud of Darry and Soda for confirming to the judge that Dally was a "real good buddy of [theirs]" (p..168). What is risky about Darry and Soda's testimony? Do you think being loyal is worth the risk? *(The judge might have considered Dally, with his criminal record, a bad influence and a sign of irresponsibility on Darry's part. As a result, the judge could have sent Ponyboy to a foster home. Answers will vary.)*

6. Why is Two-Bit relieved when Ponyboy picks up broken glass from the street? Discuss your opinion on whether Ponyboy should get tough in order to avoid being hurt. *(When Ponyboy challenges the three Socs with a broken bottle, Two-Bit worries that Ponyboy is becoming "tough" like the rest of the gang. Picking up glass demonstrates that Ponyboy is still sensitive and not a hardened hood. Answers will vary. Discussion could include how being tough and holding in his emotions certainly did not help Dally.)*

7. What does Darry mean when he says, "you don't just stop living because you lose someone" (p. 173)? *(Answers will vary. Darry is telling Ponyboy that life continues after the loss of a loved one. Though he misses Johnny and Dally, Ponyboy must move forward and make the most of his life. Quitting school will not help Ponyboy or honor Johnny and Dally.)*

8. How does Soda help keep his family together? *(Soda understands both sides in Darry and Ponyboy's arguments and can explain each brother's viewpoint to the other. Soda also reminds his brothers that they are each other's only family and therefore must stick together. As the middleman, Soda is a buffer between his brothers and also, because of their love for him, has the power to unite the family.)*

9. Analyze Soda's assertion: "If you don't have anything, you end up like Dallas…and I don't mean dead, either. I mean like he was before. And that's worse than dead" (p. 176). What might Soda mean by this, and do you agree with him? *(Answers will vary. Soda enjoys life despite its hardships. He cannot imagine being like Dally, who hardened himself in order to not feel anything and took great risks because he felt he had nothing to lose. Despite Dally's love for Johnny, or perhaps because of it, Dally died violently and tragically. Soda loved Dally, but he feels as though Dally was already dead because his upbringing made him too wary to love or trust anyone.)*

10. How well is Ponyboy recuperating? How does finding Johnny's letter help him? *(Ponyboy knows that he is in denial about Johnny's death. He finally admits that he knows Johnny is dead and that Johnny was the one who killed Bob. He realizes how rare of a friend Johnny was. However, Ponyboy cannot forget that Johnny did not want to die. Knowing Johnny no longer regretted dying and thought sacrificing his life was worth saving the children might bring Ponyboy some peace. Johnny's letter also inspires Ponyboy to write about his experiences in order to help others. By telling the story from the greasers' point of view, Ponyboy will encourage other boys in similar situations and hopefully make people think twice before judging a boy solely by his appearance, his friends, or his environment. Johnny's letter gives Ponyboy a sense of closure, a positive purpose, and a push to dream of a bright future.)*

11. Explain the significance of the first line of Ponyboy's English paper. *(Answers will vary. Ponyboy's English paper begins with the same sentence as the novel, which brings the story full circle and creates a satisfying ending. Readers now understand that Ponyboy's direct addresses throughout the novel are most likely due to his writing the story after the events take place. He had time to put events into perspective, resulting in a better connection with readers. The story within a story adds an interesting twist to the novel.)*

Supplementary Activities

1. Civics: Research the juvenile justice system in your state. Prepare a list of interview questions, and then invite a representative of the juvenile justice system to your class to answer the questions.

2. Personal Narrative: Soda says, "I'm the middleman in a tug o' war and I'm being split in half" (p. 175). Write about a time when you were caught in the middle between family or friends.

3. Comprehension: Make a list of things that are "gold." Share your list with the class, and explain your choices.

4. Character Analysis: Complete the Bio-poem on page 30 of this guide.

5. Critical Thinking: Read "speaking with S. E. Hinton…" at the end of the novel. Then, complete one of the following: (a) Write three questions you would ask the author about *The Outsiders* or (b) Write a paragraph telling the author about your feelings while reading the novel.

Post-reading Discussion Questions

1. Why is the novel titled *The Outsiders*? At the end of the novel, which characters are still outsiders? *(The novel's main character, Ponyboy, is a greaser, and the story is told from his point of view. The greasers are the outsiders in society. They want to belong and be accepted; however, society treats greasers as outcasts, causing others to judge them more harshly than Socs despite similarities shared by individuals from both groups. Ponyboy feels like an outsider not only from society but also from his gang and his family, who do not understand him because he is different. Johnny's encouragement and Cherry's and Randy's admissions of feeling different give Ponyboy the courage to reach out to other outsiders. The title also implies that everyone—greasers, Socs, and those in between—knows the feeling of being an outsider. Answers will vary.)*

2. What role do stereotypes play in the novel? *(Answers will vary. Stereotypes determine society's views of both Socs and greasers, and the unfairness of such views drives the plot of the story. For example, if Ponyboy and Johnny felt they would have been judged fairly they might not have run away after Bob's death, which would have greatly changed the story. Hatred caused by class divisions motivates characters, resulting in escalating violence throughout the story. Most Socs feel superior to the greasers, who see themselves as underprivileged failures. Yet, when stereotypes are overlooked, individuals such as Ponyboy, Cherry, and Randy make connections that bridge the gap between social classes. Dally chose to embrace his stereotype, leading to his demise.)*

3. What do you think was the author's goal in writing this novel? Does knowing S. E. Hinton was a teenager when she wrote *The Outsiders* affect your opinion of the novel? *(Answers will vary. The author wishes to show the futility of gang rivalry, to demonstrate that violence only leads to more violence, and to warn readers against judging others. Also presented are the messages that people are more alike than they think and that we all feel like outsiders at times. Some students may find possible weaknesses in plot development. Others will be impressed with the strong characterization and insight into the teen psyche.)*

4. What traits make a character heroic? Which character in the novel do you think acts the most heroic? the least? *(Answers will vary. Traits should include courage, compassion, loyalty, and strong moral values. Ponyboy supports his gang in the rumble even though he believes the only reason to fight is self-defense, he willingly rushes into the burning church to rescue trapped children, and he chooses to tell the greasers' side of the story to help other outsiders and to prevent society from judging people by their looks or social status. Darry puts his own dreams aside to work two jobs to support his brothers after their parents' deaths. Johnny shows courage when he defends Cherry and Marcia against Dally, rescues Ponyboy and himself from the Socs, decides to turn himself in to the police, sacrifices his life to save children from the fire, and motivates Ponyboy toward a better life. Dally, despite his harshness to avoid being hurt, protects his friends, from taking the blame when Two-Bit breaks school windows to helping Johnny and Ponyboy hide after Bob's death. Cherry puts honesty above loyalty in her attempt to ease tensions between Socs and greasers. With the exception of Cherry, the Socs do not display many heroic traits. Even though Randy does not participate in the rumble and makes efforts to connect with Ponyboy, he and his friends abandon Bob's body and the Socs continue to gang up on greasers in rumbles.)*

5. What does Ponyboy learn about himself during the story? Which events affect him most? *(Ponyboy realizes that he must try to understand Darry, that he should have supported Soda during his heartbreak over Sandy, and that family relationships sometimes involve struggle. Ponyboy learns that, instead of resenting being underprivileged, he can, with determination, succeed despite the hardships in his life. He needs to be tough like Darry yet sensitive like Johnny to change the negative in his life. Ponyboy is influenced by fear of being attacked by Socs, discipline issues with Darry, contemplating Cherry's and the Socs' points of view, hiding with Johnny after Bob's death, the threat of being sent to a boys' home, coping with Johnny's and Dally's deaths, etc.)*

6. How would the story be different if Johnny had not died? *(Answers will vary. Discussion should cover the following: Without Johnny's encouragement, Ponyboy may have continued being a loner and never have wanted a better life. He may have taken longer to appreciate the splendor of life. Johnny would most likely have eventually lost Dally, his hero, to a violent death and had to face the pain of such a loss.)*

7. What is the importance of setting in *The Outsiders*? Do you think the novel has the same effect on readers today as it did in 1967? *(Separation between the East Side and the West Side mirrors the story's conflict between the greasers and Socs. While the story could take place in any city, the author believes Ponyboy's unnamed city in Oklahoma, as opposed to New York or Los Angeles, makes* The Outsiders *an "everyman's story." Answers will vary. The emotional aspects and universal appeal of the novel will affect today's readers the same; however, the violence will not have the same shock value as in 1967.* The Outsiders *was a forerunner in the genre of realistic fiction that young adults enjoy today.)*

8. Discuss the significance of Robert Frost's poem, "Nothing Gold Can Stay," in the novel. *(Answers will vary. The poem implies that youthful innocence cannot last forever. Ponyboy and Johnny connect through the poem, using it to understand the tragedies in their lives. When Johnny tells Ponyboy to "stay gold," he means to always value the good things in life, appreciate the small things, and live life to the fullest.)*

9. What are the themes in the novel? Explain which one you feel is the most important and why. *(Answers will vary. Suggested themes: isolation, identity, self-esteem, society and class, relationships, violence, death, loyalty, honor, appearances, bullying, making choices, coming of age.)*

10. Explain the symbolism of the following in the novel: hair, cars, switchblades, and sunsets. Can you identify other symbols in the novel? *(Long, greased hair symbolizes the greasers' identity as a group. When Ponyboy and Johnny change their hair, they become open to non-greaser perspectives, such as fighting being useless and Socs being normal people, too. Darry's short hair may represent his desire to be more Soc-like. Cars are symbols of the Socs' wealth and represent danger to the vulnerable greasers traveling by foot. Two-Bit's switchblade symbolizes a disregard for authority. Sunsets symbolize a connection between Ponyboy and Cherry and between greasers and Socs. Answers will vary. Possible symbols include: Bob's rings [the power behind wealth and the misuse of such power]; Soda's horse, Mickey Mouse [the innocence of youth]; the country [an ideal place without stereotypes or violence].)*

11. A motif is a recurring element, object, or concept that symbolizes the central idea behind a theme. Can you identify any motifs in the novel? *(Answers will vary. References to works of literature recur throughout the novel referring to themes of social classes, coming of age, and honor. Ponyboy compares himself to Pip in Charles Dickens'* Great Expectations*, as Pip and Ponyboy are both poor orphans. Robert Frost's poem "Nothing Gold Can Stay" implies that youth and innocence do not last forever. Johnny compares the Southern gentlemen in Margaret Mitchell's* Gone with the Wind *to Dally. Later, Ponyboy compares both Johnny's and Dally's gallantry to the Southern gentlemen, and he leaves the novel unfinished like Johnny's life. Other motifs include Ponyboy's pretending or dreaming as a way to cope with difficult situations, descriptions of eyes reflecting characters' personalities or emotions, and chocolate cake representing the family bond between Ponyboy and his brothers.)*

12. Compare your definition of a "gang" with your classmates' definitions (see Initiating Activity #2 on page 6 of this guide). Where would Ponyboy's gang fit into the social system in your school? *(Answers will vary. Discussion could cover the differences between clubs and gangs, why people form different groups, and who determines to which group a person belongs.)*

13. What have you learned about appearances from reading the novel? *(Answers will vary. Appearances can identify a person or group; however, appearances can also be misleading. Long, slicked-back hair defines the greasers, yet it also affects how society judges them. The Socs who start the fights in the novel avoid punishment because they dress well and drive nice cars, while the greasers are considered hoods based on their looks and where they live.* The Outsiders *asks readers to judge greasers—and all humans—by actions rather than appearance.)*

14. Some public schools banned *The Outsiders* from classroom use because the novel contains violence and death and the main characters smoke, drink, and swear. Do you think the novel is suitable for classroom use? Why or why not? *(Answers will vary. Discussion should cover how violence and offensive subject matter add authenticity to the story, helping readers to understand what the characters and many real-life people face. Students may point out that they see violent scenes and hear swearing in movies and on TV anyway. Some students may feel the novel is not suitable for classroom use, while most will appreciate the novel for its positive messages, especially that teenagers can overcome hardships and determine the course of their lives.)*

Post-reading Extension Activities

Writing

1. Compare and contrast Dally's personality with Bob's personality. Write about how stereotypes affect each character.

2. Write a newspaper editorial about good parenting skills. Use Darry's experiences from the novel as an anecdote in your article.

3. S. E. Hinton became known as "The Voice of the Youth" after writing about the social situation in her high school. Write a story of at least 850 words about the social groups at your school.

4. Write a poem about being an "outsider."

Viewing/Speaking

5. View the 1983 movie, *The Outsiders*, and compare and contrast the movie with the novel.

6. Find a current news story that relates to a theme from *The Outsiders*. Present an oral report that summarizes the article and explains how it relates to the novel.

Drama

7. Organize a classroom debate. Choose teams to support the viewpoints of Socs and greasers. Debate solutions to resolve the gangs' differences without using violence.

Music

8. Research popular music from the 1960s. Choose three to five songs that the Socs most likely would listen to, and do the same for the greasers. Explain your choices in a brief essay.

9. Choose ten important scenes from *The Outsiders*. Create your own soundtrack for the novel by choosing a song from the 1960s that corresponds with each scene.

Art

10. Create a diorama or poster of Ponyboy meeting Cherry at the drive-in movie.

11. Design a new cover for *The Outsiders*, and write a new blurb for the back cover.

12. Summarize the novel in a computer presentation. Include graphics of characters, setting, main events, symbols, and themes.

Research

13. Write a report about today's gangs. Explain why juveniles join gangs and the risks they face by doing so. Include advice about the ways a friend or parent can prevent a teen from becoming a gang member.

14. Compare and contrast the conflict between the Socs and greasers with another example from history where one group thought it was better than another group.

15. Research the genre "bildungsroman." Then, explain whether you think *The Outsiders* could be included in this category. Include specific criteria that led to your conclusion.

Assessment for *The Outsiders*

Assessment is an ongoing process. The following ten items can be completed during the novel study. Once finished, the student and teacher will check the work. Points may be added to indicate the level of understanding.

Name _____ Date _____

Student   **Teacher**

_____   _____   1. Complete the Story Map on page 31 of this guide.

_____   _____   2. Skim the novel to find an example of each of the following literary devices: flashback, foreshadowing, idiom, onomatopoeia, simile.

_____   _____   3. Complete the Character Web on page 32 of this guide for a character other than Ponyboy. On a separate sheet of paper, explain your chosen character's relationship with Ponyboy.

_____   _____   4. Choose a favorite or important quotation from the novel. Then, complete the Using Dialogue activity on page 33 of this guide.

_____   _____   5. Write an essay about bullying based on what you learned from the novel. Discuss the reasons some people become bullies and your ideas on how to stop bullying.

_____   _____   6. Write a poem about an important theme or symbol from the novel.

_____   _____   7. Complete the Rainstorming activity on page 34 of this guide.

_____   _____   8. Summarize what you think the author's goals were for writing *The Outsiders*. Explain what the author did that made you reach your conclusions.

_____   _____   9. Complete the Rate This Novel activity on page 35 of this guide. Explain whether or not you would recommend the novel to other readers.

_____   _____   10. Correct all quizzes and tests taken over the course of the novel.

I Predict...

Directions: Spend a few minutes looking at the cover of the novel and flipping through its pages. What can you predict about the characters, the setting, and the problem in the novel? Write your predictions in the spaces below.

The Characters	The Setting	The Problem

From the information you gathered above, do you think you will enjoy reading this novel? Circle your response on the scale below.

0 —— 1 —— 2 —— 3 —— 4 —— 5 —— 6 —— 7 —— 8 —— 9 —— 10

I will not like this novel.   I will really like this novel.

Explain your prediction on the lines below.

_____

_____

_____

_____

_____

_____

_____

Word Map

Directions: Complete the word map below for each of your chosen vocabulary words.

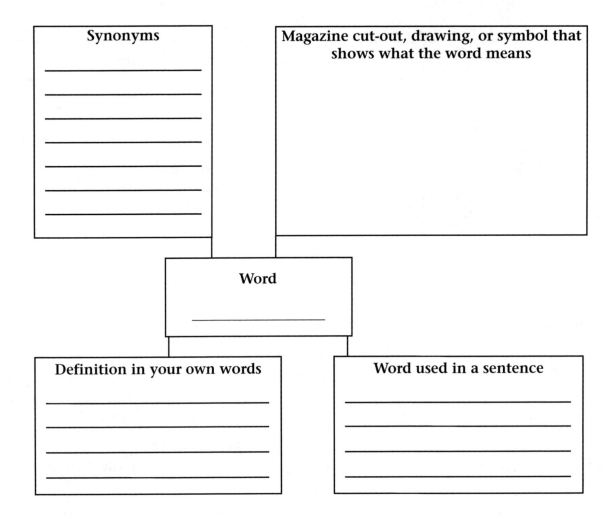

Qualities of a Hero

Directions: Choose Ponyboy, Johnny, or Dally. For each quality listed in the left column, tell if the character has this quality. If you write "yes" in the second column, then you must list an event in the third column that proves that the character has the quality. If you write "no" in the second column, you may leave the third column blank.

Quality	Does the character have this quality? (yes or no)	Event from the Story
honesty		
fairness		
bravery		
kindness		
calmness		
intelligence		
loyalty		

Look at the chart you filled in above. Based on this information, do you think the character is a hero? Explain your decision on the lines below.

_____

_____

_____

_____

_____

Bio-poem

Directions: Using the format below, write a bio-poem about Ponyboy. Then, write a bio-poem about yourself using the same format. Write a paragraph describing the values and characteristics you share.

—Line 1: First name only
—Line 2: Lover of (list three things character loves)
—Line 3: Giver of (list three things character gives)
—Line 4: Needs (list three things character needs)
—Line 5: Wants (list three things character wants)
—Line 6: Is good at (list three things character is good at)
—Line 7: Should work on (list three things character needs to improve)
—Line 8: Is similar to (list three people or other characters to whom this character is similar and list a reason behind each character)
—Line 9: Survivor of (list three things the character survives)
—Line 10: Last name only

Title _____

1. _____

2. _____

3. _____

4. _____

5. _____

6. _____

7. _____

8. _____

9. _____

10. _____

Story Map

Directions: Fill in each box below with information about the novel.

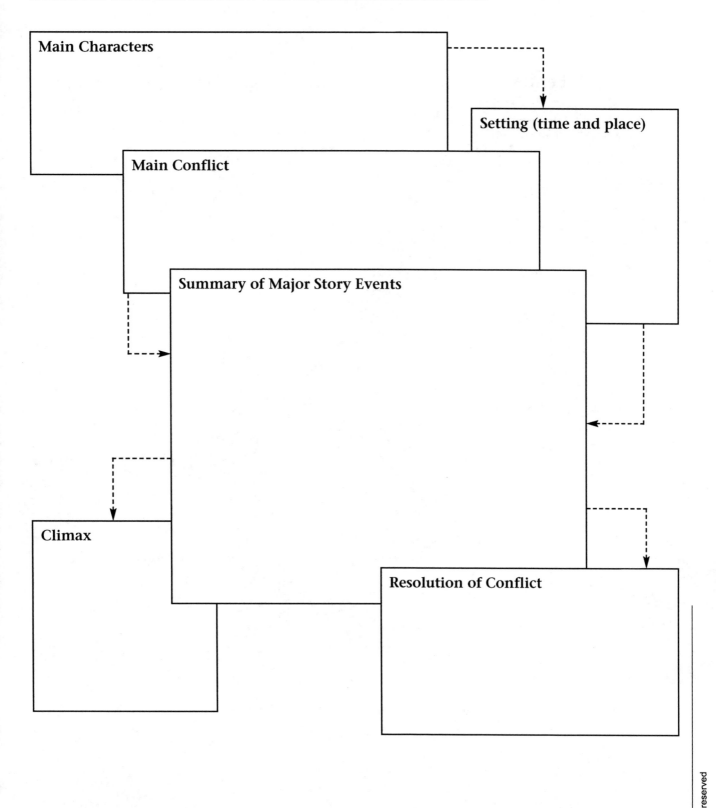

Main Characters

Setting (time and place)

Main Conflict

Summary of Major Story Events

Climax

Resolution of Conflict

Character Web

Directions: Complete the attribute web by filling in information specific to a character in the novel.

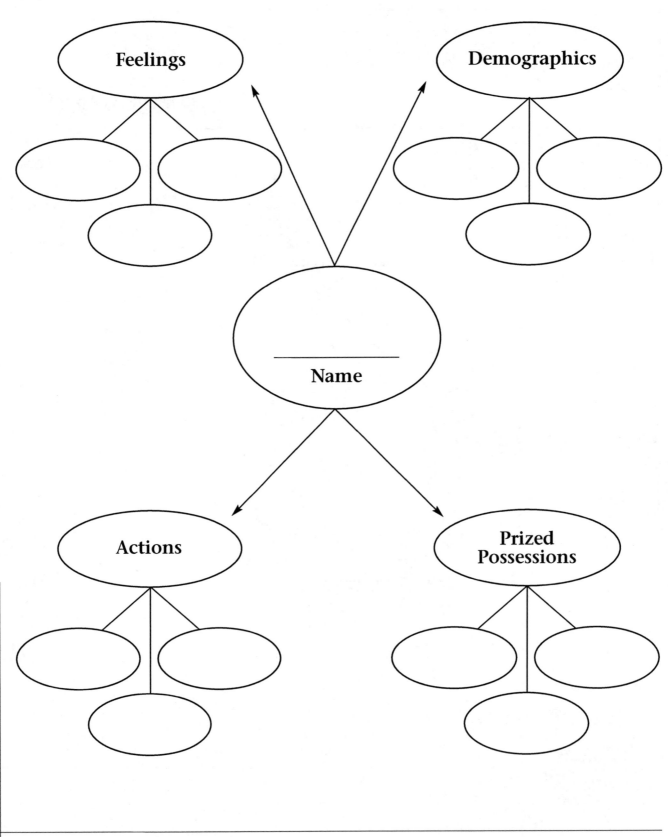

Using Dialogue

Directions: Choose some dialogue from the novel. Fill in the chart to evaluate the purpose of the dialogue and whether or not it is effective in moving along the plot.

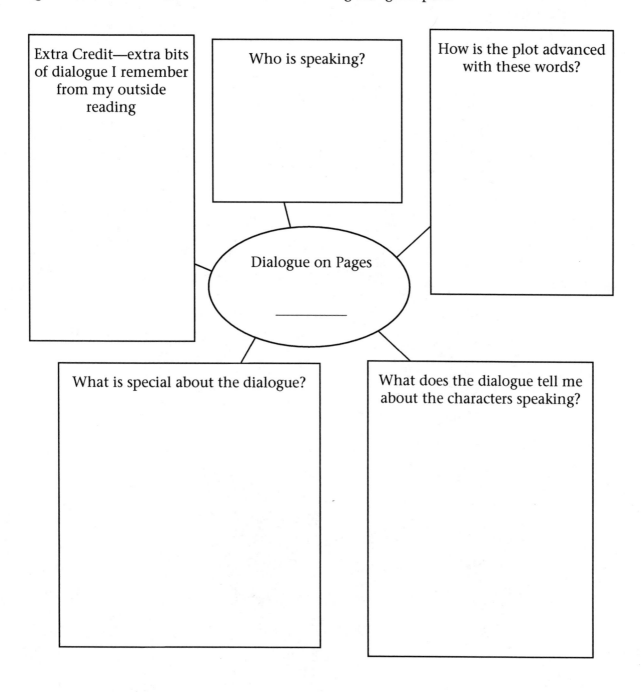

Extra Credit—extra bits of dialogue I remember from my outside reading

Who is speaking?

How is the plot advanced with these words?

Dialogue on Pages

_____

What is special about the dialogue?

What does the dialogue tell me about the characters speaking?

Rainstorming

Directions: Use the clouds below to track the effects of Ponyboy meeting Cherry Valance. Use the clouds on the left to show effects on the greasers. Use the clouds on the right to show effects on the Socs.

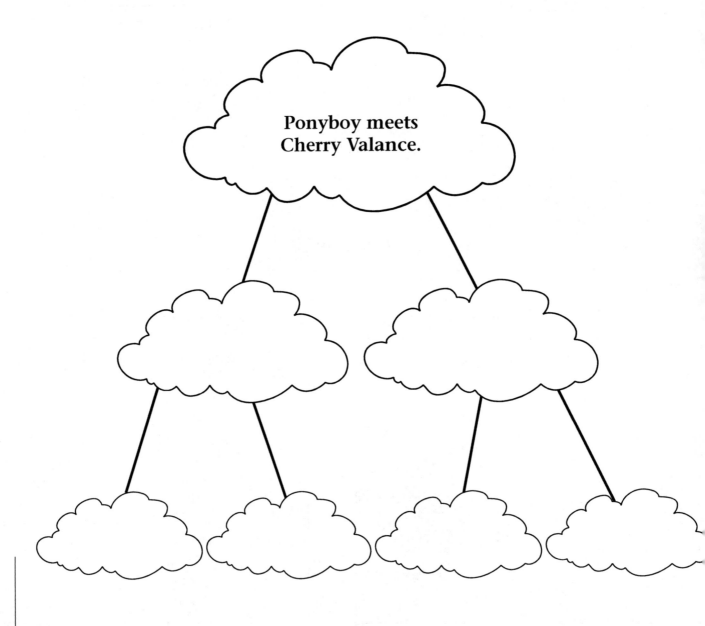

Ponyboy meets Cherry Valance.

Rate This Novel

Directions: How would you rate this novel? How clear were its ideas and characters? Use the scale below to respond to each item. Discuss your answers with the class.

1 ——————— 2 ——————— 3 ——————— 4 ——————— 5 ——————— 6
very clear   very unclear

Rating

1. description of the setting   _____

2. setting's importance   _____

3. main character's goal   _____

4. main character's problem (why he cannot reach the goal)   _____

5. main character's plan to solve the problem   _____

6. main character's thoughts   _____

7. description of secondary characters   _____

8. small details of the story   _____

9. resolution of the problem at the end of the novel   _____

10. novel's main message   _____

Linking Novel Units® Lessons to National and State Reading Assessments

During the past several years, an increasing number of students have faced some form of state-mandated competency testing in reading. Many states now administer state-developed assessments to measure the skills and knowledge emphasized in their particular reading curriculum. The discussion questions and post-reading questions in this Novel Units® Teacher Guide make excellent open-ended comprehension questions and may be used throughout the daily lessons as practice activities. The rubric below provides important information for evaluating responses to open-ended comprehension questions. Teachers may also use scoring rubrics provided for their own state's competency test.

Please note: The Novel Units® Student Packet contains optional open-ended questions in a format similar to many national and state reading assessments.

Scoring Rubric for Open-Ended Items

3-Exemplary
Thorough, complete ideas/information
Clear organization throughout
Logical reasoning/conclusions
Thorough understanding of reading task
Accurate, complete response

2-Sufficient
Many relevant ideas/pieces of information
Clear organization throughout most of response
Minor problems in logical reasoning/conclusions
General understanding of reading task
Generally accurate and complete response

1-Partially Sufficient
Minimally relevant ideas/information
Obvious gaps in organization
Obvious problems in logical reasoning/conclusions
Minimal understanding of reading task
Inaccuracies/incomplete response

0-Insufficient
Irrelevant ideas/information
No coherent organization
Major problems in logical reasoning/conclusions
Little or no understanding of reading task
Generally inaccurate/incomplete response